SPENDING

Spending

POEMS

ANTHONY HOWELL

DRAWINGS BY DILYS BIDEWELL

*M*enard
*M*edames

Worldwide distribution (except North America)
Central Books/Troika 99 Wallis Road
Hackney Wick, London E9 SLN
Telephone 020 8986 4854   Fax 020 8533 5821

Distribution in North America
Small Press Distribution Inc., 1341 Seventh Street
Berkeley, CA 94710, USA

ISBN 1 874320 27 6

MENARD/MEDAMES
8 The Oaks, Woodside Avenue, London N12 8AR
Telephone and fax 020 8446 5571

For the girls and boys of 'Teenage Sex'

CONTENTS

TOPLESS

Firm full breasts,
And the beat I skip
As the woman
Wades in for a dip.

Under a hanky
On his rock,
Her lover perches,
Deep in a book.

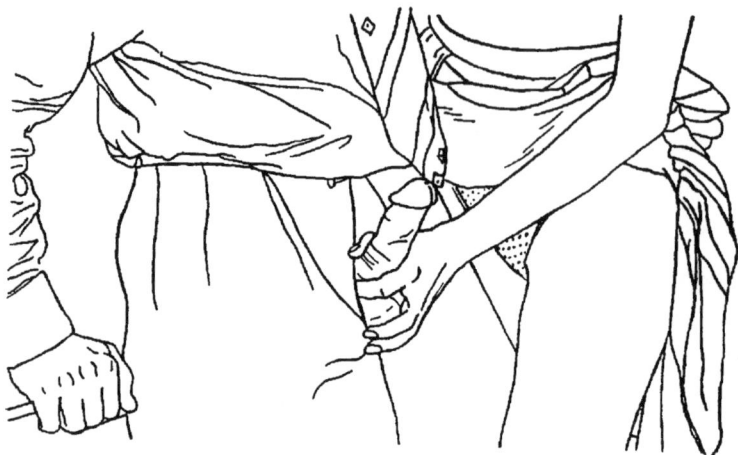

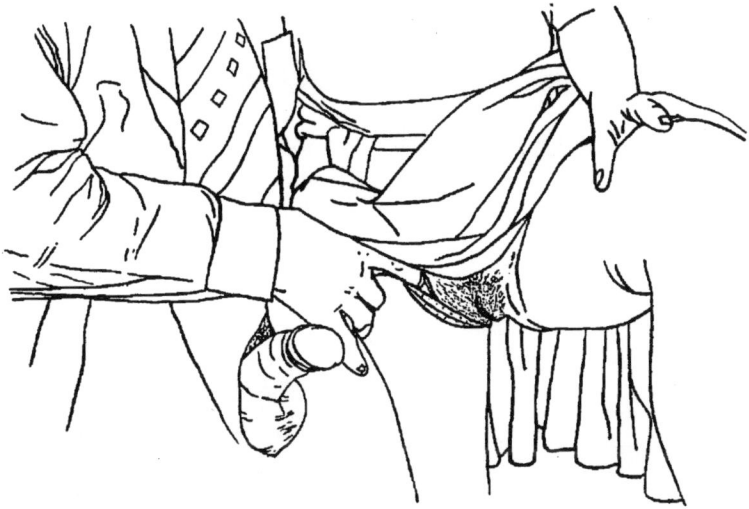

SPENDING

On top of the bargain Persian rugs,
The waistcoat and the small glass dish
With serrated edges – for my soap –
There's what I paid for Etta James

And Little Milton in the H.M.V.,
And how I spent, on Emma's pubic hair,
And what it might cost Emma to declare
How much she spent that weekend spent with me.

SHAVEN

I told her that I'd read you her description of Lobin. Absolute quiet,
Smell of figtree, breath of moon asleep in marble house . . .
I told her you had been a pig over one very small sweet fig,
A fig for making jam perhaps instead of eating loose.

I told her then I'd told you about her flagrant little fig,
And how I split its crack apart – and what I tasted there.
I told her that I'd made *you* come describing how I'd used her bum.
'Her fig's a peach but you should try her pear!'

A VISITOR

I do wish you would come and snuggle up with me!
I called as she began to climb the stairs.
And she came into my bed with nothing on
And rubbed her warm behind against my front.

I revelled in her body's milky grain,
Kissed her raspberry nipples, licked her mouth
And pushed my quick erection up inside
Her soft enclosure – next I pulled it out.

I pulled it out. I felt quite shy and speechless.
Not knowing what to whisper makes me lose it.
But then she lewdly pushed her finger into me
And I began to thank her for her rudeness

And to voice some horny thoughts till hard enough
To penetrate her body once again;
Which provoked a state which couldn't last,
But was heaven for me, as I squirted all over her tummy.

14

SUNK

Your cunt is a warm, wet darkness, a delight.
And though you are trim and twenty-two,
And though your skin is white,
Your cunt is an unsung oracle
Which spells Arcadia for me and
I enter and my orgasm wells up in me.

I need to come at once, no way to bring you off first.
And now I am trammelled in a mystery,
For you are the obverse form of Tiresias:
Female, with a beard between your legs.
How can a girl be equipped with what feels
So deep to someone very much older than she is?

Your cunt seems a lovely pool for me.
I sink into it and I grow younger,
Younger – till my crisis shakes eternity.
Really, yours is not some neat young vulva
But something wild as your head of hair
Which swirls about so – such is your vagina.

FIDO

I have watched you crawl happily like a little dog
And want to play being dogs with you.
We two should sniff our sexual regions eagerly,
Eagerly, on all fours, at the same time:

Each of us sticking our bottoms up for the other to inspect.
I want this so much that it brings me erect
Just to think about doing it next time we meet.
I daren't even look at the dogs in the street.

LOVE LETTER

My dear, how nice you looked that afternoon
When you were sleeping naked in the heat,
And I could see your lovely smooth behind
And wanted to lean over it and worship it.

I'm thinking what a randy girl I've got,
And what it's like to stretch out on my front
As hands and lips investigate my butt:
Of course this makes me stiffen, and I bend

My prick and push it in between my legs
For you to get a grip on from the back.
I'm pleased you've chosen me to be your champ
And want to put a pillow underneath you,

Seize you, spread you, have you from the rump,
According you the pleasure of my penis
While I suck your tongue. When that's allowed,
Your lover knows you're quite as rude as he is.

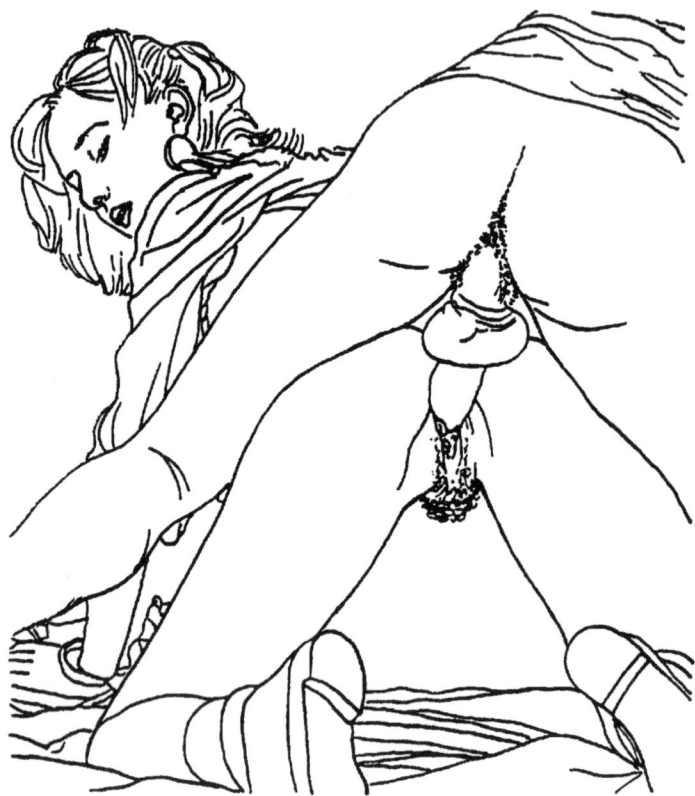

PURDAH

A leather jacket and an ankle-length
Camouflage skirt give me the strength
To say fuck it, we'll go out.
These protect me from the dirt
Projected by intrusive eyes
Crepitating cruelties at the sight
Of my hour-glass figure and the metal
In my nostrils, but at night,
Naked and soft on the low bed
In your loft, it thrills me
To reveal the fineness of my fettle.

MADRIGAL

When it rains the rooms go very dark.
Her bust shakes when she laughs
In her loose tee-shirt.
'Be careful, I'm fertile,' she says,
Taking me in hand.
And then, above her pubic hair,
The semen I spill over her
Lies glistening like spray where
It's blown off waves onto sand.

ACROSTIC

Bending
Over
Touching
Toes
Obediently
Meek.

EPIGRAM

Maybe she's aware
That I'm listening,
But she doesn't care.
And later on,
When he's gone,
She'll part her dressing-gown,
And oh how magical
To sniff him there.

HAIKU

Don't wait up.
She's gone off to fuck
Like the rabbit
She looks enough like.

EPITAPH

Take her for a coffee then
In Bab's beastly bistro,
Where the Tiger sauce has dripped
Into your raffia table-mat
– Looks like crusted shit.
Harlots have been murdered where you sit.
The bitterness of poor quality remains
Long after the sweetness of low price is forgotten.

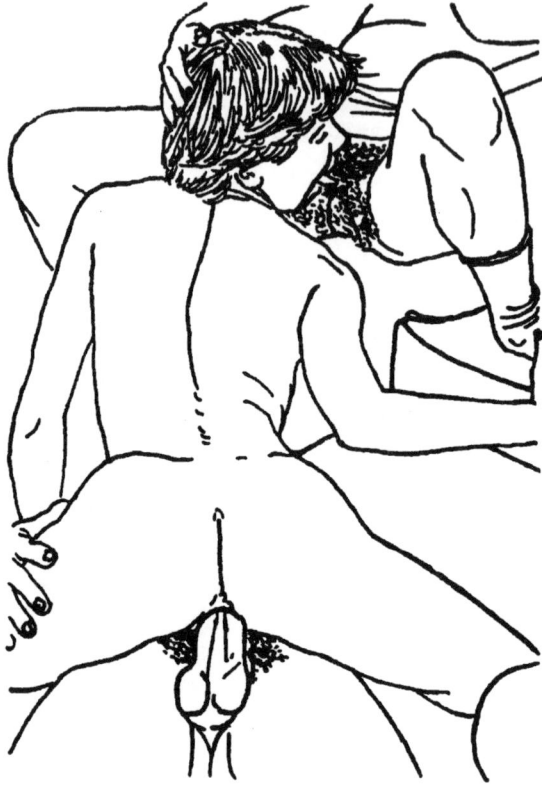

CLIENTELE

As for the gentleman,
He is a clown.
The taxi spouts through the top of his head
With a bang.

Men get worked up so quickly
And then – whoosh –
That's the battle over with
For half an hour or more.
Generally more, don't let them kid you
– Unless they've just come out of the nick,
And then they're like a runny cold all night;
A bit wobbly after the third one
But still up to it.

ONE AFTERNOON

Rain blew over the roof again.
Both of our blokes were on
A continental lorry run.
I ran my tongue along her teeth.

Men are funny, girls are lovely
In miniskirts and the right circumstances anyway.
Call it deprivation
– With a touch of what
She likes to sprinkle everywhere.
I smelled my fingers a lot
After she left.

ANY EXCUSE

Piled on the bed, she asks you to anoint each hurt arena:
Sooth her seething bites, her peelings; salve her stings
From bellying medusae. Oh, but you spread the worm you squeeze
With care embalming burns like those that salmonise her throat.

And here your finger shapes her nose. Or you may work your way
Around each other: cleansing salty pores, turning over,
Basted, being turned. You need to sense the seams beneath
– The geology of fibres – as you saturate the skin with lotions,

Oiling the shins, the elbows; rubbing cocoa butter into scars.
Then straddling her waist you knead the palpable
Dough of the north into sumptuous shape, blending it with
Aloe vera, camomile and the tea-tree of the south.

Wending your way down her keyboard you finally
Activate buttocks gone slack. Nice closing these and parting these,
Exposing the wet, available reason, and bringing your slippery
Stiffening up against it as the girl sighs and hollows her back.

ITINERARY

Something like Arpège, I trace
The source of it back to her nape
As she bends in bronzed silhouette
To study her maps.

A blue dress with polka dots.
She is working out her route at the table
Next to me. Her tall glass gets lifted
And the day swells like yeast from the bakery.

I want to travel around her neck
And go with her into the mountains but
The journey from my table to hers
Is just too tricky to negotiate.

TIRE-BOUCHON

You weren't equipped to walk,
When first I got you under me,
And me, I pulled the cork
On a rouge of fine bouquet;
Came inside you twice,
Deflowered your renown,
And you too drunk to realise,
But lovely the next day
In my claret dressing-gown.

THE WAVES

She flows in and she falls apart
Or smashes herself against me,
But then she seeps away again,
Ebbing quickly, in elusive rivulets.

Ply this one with cognac. It works.
How easily her slacks come off.
But then she keeps away again.
We're just good friends. Besides, there are the cats.

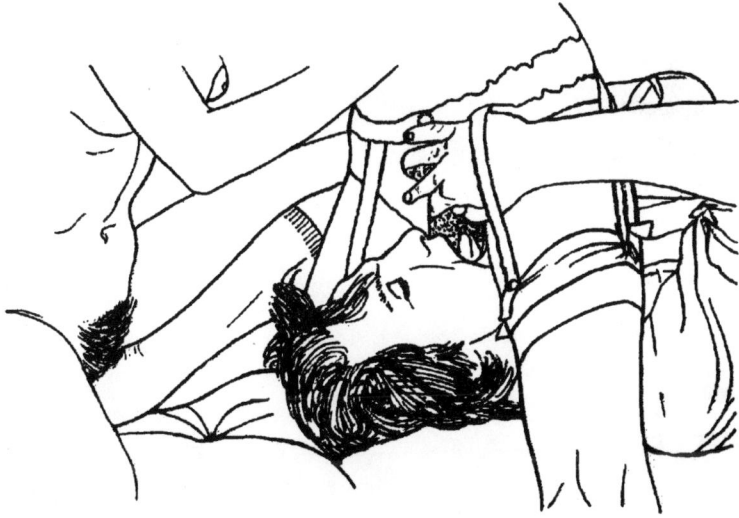

WASP

Don't cite me
Sympathy for animals
In abattoirs.

You want to keep
That waistline
Solar plexic.

Hell, there are
Plenty of hard bodies
Like yours:

Immaculate,
And later anorexic.

AUTO

It's easy enough to construct for yourself a crackpot situation
Whereby you can confidently say to someone, 'Orgasm?
What's special about an orgasm for chrissake? An orgasm,
It's just like having a pee.' So slake your tension privately,
But I dare you to resist that option for a while and see
If it doesn't lead to a hankering for some conclusive paroxysm
Which might break you up. The trouble is you've no desire to be
Broken up – you're far more keen on keeping an
Avowed image intact – and why not? So toss and turn apart,
Seeming self-sufficient – keeping restive distance
Between you and prospective types you may not want to hurt.

A BEAUTY

She hates how they inhale
As she passes,
Flinches as they scratch her
With their eyes.

And my taste
Gets into her clothing,
Her underwear,
And she can smell me

Watching her.

A SPELL

If she has to lie beside her man, let her surreptitiously touch
      herself in the dark, longing to whisper my name.
When he climbs on top of her, let her wish it was me mounting her.
Let her despise his penis, let her distaste for it keep it flaccid,
      let her find its odour most unpleasant.
Let her memory of how she used my cock interfere with their intercourse.
If he tries to get into her from the back,
      let her squeeze her buttocks tight and shift away emphatically.
Let her discover that he has been seeing some pallid woman with acne.
Let her feel contempt for the man. Let her reflect on her pity for him.
      Let her learn to disdain it.
Let the mere thought of his come make her unspeakably bad-tempered.
Let her feel revulsion at the state of his clothing,
      loathing at the sound of his eating.
Let her fingers touch her body here and there,
      repeating the itinerary taken by my hands on her.
Let her feel hopeless and alone when obliged to sit on the sofa
      watching television with that man.
Let her find any excuse to come back to me just as soon as she can.

ANTILOVE

Why can't you come? Why can't you come when
We last forever in bed?
                              Because love doesn't
Unfasten me now – it's too social, the thing done.
As if one weren't to be used, and shamefully too.

Don't fondle too fondly. It can disagree
With liking to shame – your likes exciting me.
Love's special perhaps, respected, pleasant.
But I can get further with the readers' letters

And my own digit. Mention
No heavenly choir. Found with another
Girl or a boy with my knickers down in
A crude way at the office – that might do it.

Choosing to imagine us as if we'd never met
Before turns me on more than the tenderness
Of deep feeling etcetera.
                              Me too. I much prefer
Some rude experience kids get up to.

I can't bear that violin within a negligée,
False adult innocence, advertised togetherness.
I like it more illicit, more extreme or strict,
Wielding the strap for a stain at your gusset,

Doing what is dangerous, voicing the obscene.
For if I whisper names and say you fancy them,
You signal the beginnings of your orgasm,
Though such beginnings make me come too soon.

TRACY

Nothing yet can make my heart beat faster
Than when Tracy tells me she's been naughty.
I insist she has to call me 'Master'
And will soon display her at a party.

Master will demand that she undress,
And Tracy will comply in front
Of fully-clothed men and women bent
On savouring her abject state of readiness.

Next he will ask her kindly to reveal
Her useable regions – *and* she will do it.
The women will gather behind her to feel
Her buttocks and explore her slit.

They'll point out that it's really rather wet,
Then unzip the trousers of the men,
Harden their pricks and guide them one
After another up the little slut.

ASTONISHMENT

I know how much you love to whisper crude
Scenarios which work like some hot dream
On my desires, and as I touch my clit
You kiss me, then you mention her by name,
Talk about her plump, inviting bum
And how you make her malleable and wet.

I know you like imagining you're fucking her
When actually you're drenching me with come,
But then you say you call her by *my* name
Just before you flood your little Miss
And that you feel extremely rude
And cruel too to act like this.

I know you'd love it if we'd let you bed
Us both together. Very keen to spout,
After we'd both sucked it for a bit,
Your prick would prod and poke her pretty slit,
And then I'd watch it sliding in and out
Till you let fly and she cried Oh my God!

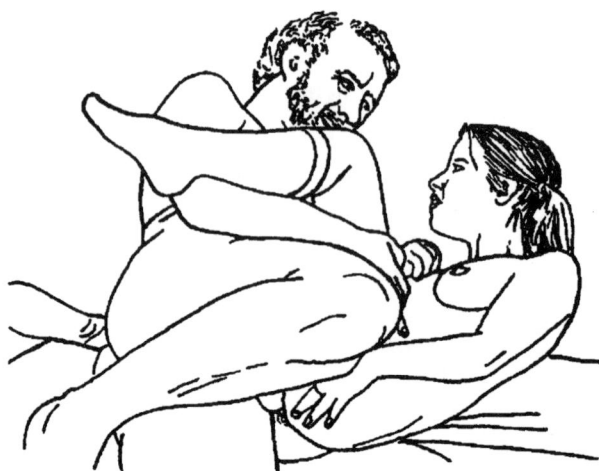

FIRST LOVE

My father calls it 'our forsaken spot'.
We go there when he's troubled by his itch.
It's where he kneels to rid me of my frock
Then turn me round and spread me so as to sniff
Me as he swears he would a rose. A ditch
Goes trickling through the thicket where I squat
Over the monster he says is a cock,
And I feel all grown up, and proud
That I can take so much of it inside.
I tell him this, and he laughs aloud
And lists the bits of me worth kisses if
He strips me like a willow. He has called
Me sweetheart too, his special, secret bride.
My front is hairless and his head is bald.

COMPLAINT OF THE PAGE

I felt coerced into a complicity with the pen,
And when it was over I was the only witness
To the indecency perpetrated upon me.
Now it's the shame I find damaging, not so much
Of being compelled to bear the inscription
As of the joy experienced in the act
Despite my wishes. That is inadmissible.
Had I remained unmoved, I could have scorned
The issue and erased it, but
Since the instrument not only forced itself
Upon me but also snatched away
My ability to respond with appropriate blankness,
I have been transformed into a slut
Worthy of nothing but this dirty treatment.
Can't you see the rapist is inside me?

THE GUIDING GLOVE

One pampered by a slave
May condescend to give
The orders which it proves
Her pleasure to obey;

But he may start to crave
The mastery she suits
And find it hard to live
Without her being tied

To his aloof demands.
And so, from pulling boots,
She graduates to calling
Many of the shots,

While he becomes a tried
And tested master, falling
More beneath her spell
With every serviced lust:

Putty in her hands,
A potentate whose duty
It must be to serve
The needs of her serene

Connivance in his aims,
As with a pillow thrust
Beneath her she provokes
Indelicate attack,

Or, bossily abject,
Relieves him of his nectar,
Ruling his desires
By insisting on his rules;

Compliably prepared
To lead him by the sceptre
Into darker lairs
Than he would have her enter.

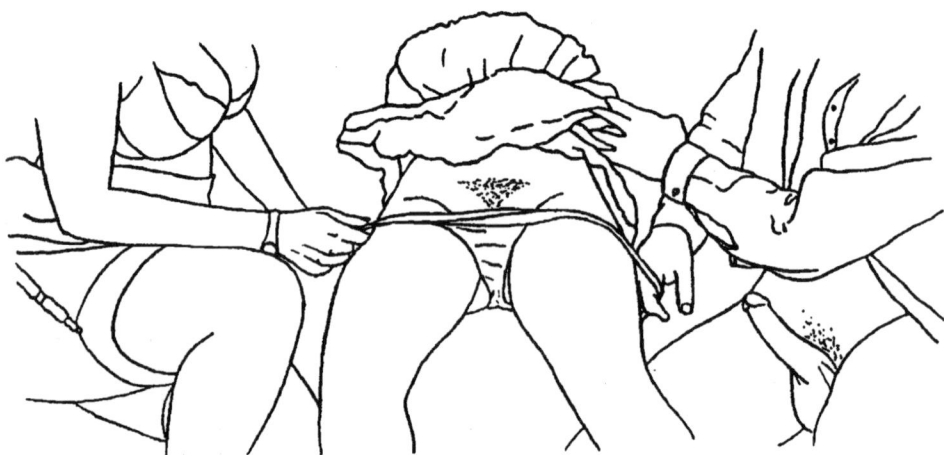

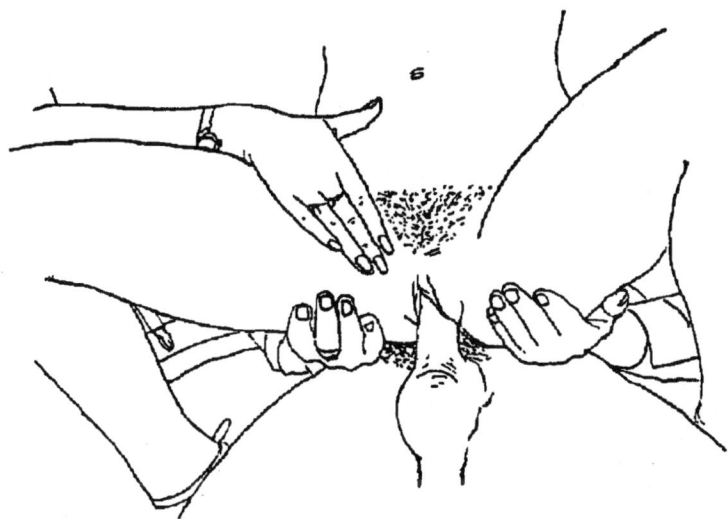

A MYSTERY

What goads me to apply
My pelvis to his thigh,
And why should I submit
To his fingering my slit?

Must I lewdly voice
The fancy of my choice
As his boxers offer bliss
To my clitoris?

How can I abide
Him poking from the side
And slowing down his rate
While I masturbate?

Why, when I would balk
At her sitting on his stalk,
Does the notion make me come?
Can I really be so dumb?

And when he wants to go
Where she ought to tell him no,
What makes a girl enjoy
Being buggared like a boy?

Oozing from his fuck,
I climb aboard this truck,
But how can I pretend
That our road is at an end?

AJAR

Every time I think of it
My mind goes blurry
With the utter silent sensuousness of it.
Just her high heels
Coming down with a click;
Her knuckles going white
As she gripped the sides of the table.

ANTHONY HOWELL

Anthony Howell was born in 1945. By 1965 he was a
dancer with the Royal Ballet, but soon after he left
the ballet to concentrate on writing. In 1973, he was
invited to join the Program for International Writers
at the University of Iowa. In 1975, his erotic text,
Oslo: A Tantric Ode, was published by Calder and
Boyars. Since then his output has included many
collections of poetry and a novel, *In the Company of
Others*, published in 1986. Howell was the founder of
The Theatre of Mistakes, and under his direction
the company made notable appearances all over the
world. In 1995 he performed his *Commentary on
Klein* with several naked performers during the Yves
Klein exhibition at the Hayward Gallery. In 1997 he
was short-listed for a Paul Hamlyn Award,
and recently he has performed upside
down and back to front
with a pair of pigs.

DILYS BIDEWELL

Dilys Bidewell was born in Sydney, Australia, in 1954. It was here she pursued her interest in drawing whilst practising as an architect, and first collaborated with Anthony Howell on a series of drawings for his performance, *The Tower*, which were exhibited at the Art Gallery of New South Wales in 1984. In the following year she moved to London, and in 1990 her work was seen in the New Contemporaries exhibition and in the Post-Morality Show at Kettles Yard, Cambridge.

Recently her drawings have been exhibited
in Melbourne, Australia. She teaches
at Wimbledon School of Art.

ANTHONY HOWELL: BIBLIOGRAPHY

1968–9 *Sergei de Diaghileff* – long poem – Turret Books, London.

1969 *Inside the Castle* – poems – Barrie & Rockliff, The Cresset Press, London.

1970 *Imruil* – free translation from pre-Islamic Arabic – Barrie & Rockliff, London.

1971 Edited *Erotic Lyrics* – anthology – for Studio Vista, London.

1972 *Femina Deserta* – poem – Softly Loudly Books, London.

1975 *Oslo: a Tantric Ode* – book-length poem – Calder & Boyars, London.
Elements of Performance Art – textbook for performance artists – co-authored with Fiona Templeton, Ting Books, London.

1983 *Notions of a Mirror* – poems – Anvil Press Poetry, London.

1984 *Winter's not Gone* – poems – The Many Press, London.

1986   *Why I may never see the Walls of China* – poems – Anvil Press Poetry, London.
        In the Company of Others – novel – by Marion Boyars, London.

1990   *Howell's Law* – poems – by Anvil Press Poetry, London.

1992   Edited and introduced *Near Calvary – Selected Poems of Nicholas Lafitte* – The Many Press, London.

1995   *First Time in Japan* – poems – Anvil Press Poetry, London.

1999   *Sonnets* – Grey Suit Editions, London.
        The Analysis of Performance Art, Harwood Academic Publishers, London.

2000   *Serbian Sturgeon: Journal of a visit to Belgrade,* Harwood Academic Publishers, London.
        Selected Poems, Anvil Press, London.

THE MENARD PRESS

The Menard Press was founded in 1969. The press has published fiction, war memoirs, autobiography, literary and art criticism, and essays on disarmament, religion and kabbala – but its main concern has been poetry, in particular poetry in translation.

The year 2001 sees the launch of an associated but separate imprint, Menard Medames. The name was conceived after a dish of *foul medames* served at Gaby's in the Charing Cross Road.

It was at Gaby's early in 2000 that Anthony Howell handed over the manuscript of *Spending*, the first in a series of provocative writing and drawing to be published at irregular intervals.

Typeset in Ehrhardt by Antony Gray
Printed and bound in Great Britain by
the Alden Press, Oxford